HUNTING AND FISHING

GOING FLY-FISHING

BY FELIX PETERS

Gareth Stevens
PUBLISHING

Please visit our website, www.garethstevens.com. For a free color catalog of all our high-quality books, call toll free 1-800-542-2595 or fax 1-877-542-2596.

Cataloging-in-Publication Data
Names: Peters, Felix.
Title: Going fly-fishing / Felix Peters.
Description: Buffalo, NY : Gareth Stevens Publishing, 2027. | Series: Hunting and fishing | Includes glossary and index.
Identifiers: ISBN 9781482482584 (pbk.) | ISBN 9781482482591 (library bound) | ISBN 9781482482607 (ebook)
Subjects: LCSH: Fly fishing--Juvenile literature.
Classification: LCC SH456.P484 2027 | DDC 799.124--dc23

Published in 2027
Gareth Stevens Publishing
2544 Clinton Street
Buffalo, NY 14224

Portions of this work were originally authored by Emily Rose Oachs and published as *Fly-Fishing*. All new material in this edition was authored by Felix Peters.

Designer: Joshua Olson
Editor: Noah Riccardi

Photo credits: Cover, p. 1 bekirevren/Shutterstock.com; p. 4 Driftless Studio/iStockphoto; p. 7 duncan1890/iStockphoto; p. 8 skibreck/iStockphoto; p. 10 Matt Benoit/Shutterstock.com; p. 13 DoublePHOTO studio/Shutterstock.com; p. 14 B. W. Folsom/Shutterstock.com; p. 16 Raphael Fortier Metivier/Shutterstock.com; p. 19 Andy Bowlin/iStockphoto; p. 20 J. Kendall/iStockphoto; p. 23 creighton359/iStockphoto; pp. 24, 29 goodluz/Shutterstock.com; p. 27 wwwarjag/Shutterstock.com.

Printed in China

CPSIA compliance information: Batch #QS27GS: For further information contact Gareth Stevens at 1-800-542-2595.

TABLE OF CONTENTS

CHAPTER 1

HISTORY OF FLY-FISHING

In fly-fishing, **anglers** use **lures** known as flies. Flies are hooks tied with feathers, hair, yarn, and other materials. They are made to attract and catch fish. Flies look like the insects or small animals that fish eat. Fish swim and bite on the lure. Then, they can be reeled in. The angler pulls the fish in close, then picks it up with a net.

Fly-fishing has existed for almost 2,000 years.

People have enjoyed fly-fishing since ancient times. In 200 CE, a Roman author described people fishing with fake flies in southern Europe. Centuries later, in the early 1200s, British anglers fly-fished for trout and grayling along the banks of rivers and streams. During the next century, this method of fishing spread throughout the rest of Europe. By the late 1400s, fly-fishing was a popular sport among England's upper classes.

European immigrants brought the sport to North America. They fished the broad rivers of the continent's eastern coast. By the 1950s, the rugged American West was attracting more and more fly-fishers.

An angler fishes on the Isle of Arran in Scotland in the 1800s.

For many years, people believed that fly-fishing was a sport for only the wealthy. Fly-fishing gear can be very expensive.

An angler nets a rainbow trout.

Some high-end fly-fishing rods can cost hundreds of dollars. But there are many affordable options that work just as well. Over time, more people have learned about these other options. The sport's popularity has grown.

Fly-fishing locations have also expanded. At first, people fly-fished only in bodies of fresh water, such as rivers or streams. Later on, anglers began **casting** their lines in salt water, too.

Today, anglers enjoy fly-fishing in waters around the world. Freshwater anglers often catch steelhead, trout, grayling, and salmon. Saltwater anglers often target bonefish and tarpon.

CHAPTER 2

REELS, LINES, FLIES, AND MORE

Fly-fishing gets its name from the special lures that anglers use. These flies come in many types. Each fly is designed for a different situation. Some flies float on the surface of the water. Other flies sink into the water. Anglers usually carry many kinds of flies with them.

There are four main types of fly-fishing lures.

An angler's long fly rod launches the fly out onto the water. Fly rods also help anglers set the hook in a fish's mouth and **land** the fish. A fly rod must be both strong and flexible. This allows the rod to bend under the weight of a large fish without breaking.

TYING FLIES

Thousands of different fly patterns exist. Anglers can purchase flies from fly shops or online. Yet for many anglers, the process of tying flies can be as relaxing and enjoyable as fishing. Catching fish on flies they have tied themselves can be one of the sport's greatest rewards.

Fly-fishing rods are typically between 7 feet (2.1 m) and 11 feet (3.4 m) long.

A reel at the base of the rod stores the line. Reels can hold as much as 100 feet (30 m) of line. Fly-fishing line tends to be heavy. Its weight helps push the fly forward when anglers cast.

This allows them to send the fly farther out onto the water.

A leader connects the fly to the line. The leader gently drops the fly onto the water's surface. It also helps the fly move in the water. The leader is lightweight and difficult to see. Anglers use the leader to copy the natural movements of a fish's prey. They try to trick fish into thinking that the flies are food.

Anglers use other helpful gear, too. Sometimes anglers must wade into the water to cast to a certain area. Tall, waterproof pants called waders help them stay dry. Other anglers wear vests with many pockets. The pockets provide space

This fishing vest has a patch of fleece where anglers can store flies.

for anglers to keep tackle close at hand. Some anglers also carry **creels** for storing the fish they catch.

CHAPTER 3

MAKING THE CATCH

Choosing a good location is a key part of fly-fishing. Anglers look for places where fish are likely to feed. Weedy areas and water near plants and trees are good options. So are areas behind boulders or near fallen logs. Fish also tend to swim near **eddies** and other areas with slow currents.

Fly-fishing is a great way to explore nature.

These calmer waters help keep fish from wasting energy.

Anglers must approach their fishing spots carefully. Bright clothing or loud noises can frighten fish. Anglers often wear clothes that blend in with the fish's **habitat**. They may even crouch or crawl to the water's edge.

PLAYING A FISH

Fish often try to free themselves from hooks. Anglers must fight against the fish until they tire themselves out. This is called playing a fish. When playing a fish, an angler keeps their line tight. They keep the tip of their rod up. Once the fish is exhausted, the angler can land it.

Many anglers fish for trout.

When a fish bites, the angler quickly pulls the line tight. This sets the hook in the fish's mouth. Then the angler begins reeling the fish in closer. A net can help the angler scoop up and land the fish.

CHAPTER 4

SAFE FISHING

Fly-fishing is a great way to enjoy the outdoors. But it also brings some risks. A fly's hook is sharp enough to pierce a person's skin. Before casting, anglers should look for people nearby. This helps them avoid hooking others or getting hooked themselves.

It is important to be careful when wading.

Fast-flowing water can knock over an angler. Underwater rocks may be slippery. If a person stumbles and falls into the water, a strong current could sweep them away. The cold water could also cause them to get **hypothermia**. To prevent this, anglers should wade slowly and cautiously.

WEATHER SAFETY

Anglers must keep an eye on the weather. On clear days, anglers should wear sunscreen, hats, and sunglasses. Rain jackets and other waterproof clothing will keep them warm and dry in the rain. If a thunderstorm looms, anglers should stop fishing and seek shelter immediately. Their fly rods can conduct electricity if struck by lightning.

Wading boots help anglers keep their footing on rocky bottoms.

Walking sticks help anglers maintain their balance in the water. Secure wading belts keep water out of waders if anglers fall.

First aid kits help anglers care for minor injuries. People fishing in remote areas should also pack blankets, compasses, and extra food. This helps them be prepared in case of emergencies.

CHAPTER 5

SUSTAINABLE FISHING

Governments create fly-fishing laws to help with **conservation**. By following these laws, anglers can help protect the health of fish and their habitats. Some laws allow people to fly-fish only at certain times of year. Laws may also limit how many fish anglers can keep. Other laws require anglers to keep only fish above a certain size.

It is important to handle fish gently.

Anglers must release any fish smaller than this size. This helps make sure young fish can grow into adults and reproduce.

Fly-fishing laws also require most anglers to purchase fishing licenses. Part of the money from license sales is used to help with conservation. The government uses this money to care for the environment. The money may go toward cleaning rivers and lakes.

While fishing, anglers should be careful not to disturb the habitats of fish and other animals. They should clean up their own litter and any litter left by others.

Many anglers also choose to practice catch-and-release fishing. These anglers

Anglers make sure a fish has fully recovered before letting it go back into the water.

do not keep the fish they catch. Instead, they carefully unhook the fish. Then they gently return the fish to the water. Catch-and-release fishing helps ensure that there will be enough fish for other anglers to catch in the future.

FACT FILE

RIVERS OF MONTANA

Many people travel for fly-fishing. They look for destinations with lots of fish and with great natural scenery. In the United States, Montana is known for both.

Montana has lots of rivers with plenty of trout. Anglers come from far away to fish in its rivers. The state has large areas of mountainous land, so it's also known for its natural beauty.

The Yellowstone River is especially famous. It has more than 200 miles (320 km) of water with fish for catching. The river has lots of different sections, each with its own challenges. The Yellowstone flows through high canyons with great views. It also has zones of tough rapids. These

People often travel to Montana to fly-fish.

areas each have different kinds of fish that anglers try to catch. All of this makes the Yellowstone River in Montana an iconic fly-fishing spot.

TEST YOUR KNOWLEDGE

Take this quiz to test your knowledge.

1. Write a sentence that describes the key ideas from Chapter 5.

2. What do you think would be the most difficult part of fly-fishing? Why?

3. What piece of equipment stores the fly line?

    A. the reel
    B. the creel
    C. the leader

4. What might happen if anglers kept fish that were below the size limit?

    A. The fish population would increase because the fish would not have to compete for food.
    B. The fish population would decrease because fewer fish would survive to become adults.
    C. The fish population would stay the same because fish size and numbers are not related.

Answers can be found on page 32.

GLOSSARY

anglers
People who fish with a rod, reel, and line.

casting
Using a fishing rod to throw a line with bait or a lure out over the water.

conservation
The careful protection of plants, animals, and natural resources so they are not lost, ruined, or wasted.

creels
Baskets that anglers use to hold their fish.

eddies
Currents of water that move in a circle or flow the opposite way from the main current.

habitat
The type of place where plants or animals normally grow or live.

hypothermia
The loss of body heat to a level much lower than normal.

land
To bring in a hooked fish from the water.

lures
Types of artificial bait used to attract and catch fish.

FOR MORE INFORMATION

BOOKS

Reeves, Diane Lindsey. *Freshwater Fishing*. Minneapolis, MN: Lerner Publications, 2024.

Simons, Lisa M. Bolt. *Go Freshwater Fishing!* North Mankato, MN: Capstone Publishing, 2022.

WEBSITES

Britannica Kids: Fishing
kids.britannica.com/students/article/fishing/274328
Learn more about fishing at this site.

National Geographic Kids: Montana
kids.nationalgeographic.com/geography/states/article/montana
Learn more about Montana, a popular fly-fishing location.

Publisher's note to educators and parents: Our editors have carefully reviewed these websites to ensure that they are suitable for students. Many websites change frequently, however, and we cannot guarantee that a site's future contents will continue to meet our high standards of quality and educational value. Be advised that students should be closely supervised whenever they access the internet.

INDEX

Answer Key: 1. Answers will vary; 2. Answers will vary; 3. A; 4. B